Congratulations!
Keep the faith.

Jerry & Lorrie Foley

EXCUSE ME!

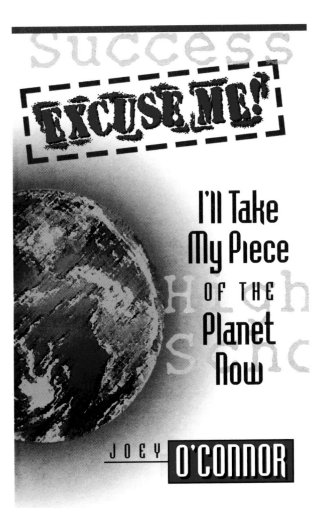

EXCUSE ME!

I'll Take My Piece of the Planet Now

JOEY O'CONNOR

Baker Books

A Division of Baker Book House Co
Grand Rapids, Michigan 49516

Published by Baker Books
a division of Baker Book House Company
P.O. Box 6287, Grand Rapids, MI 49516–6287

Printed in the United States of America

Library of Congress Cataloging-in-Publication Data

O'Connor, Joey, 1964–
    Excuse me! I'll take my piece of the planet now / Joey O'Connor.
       p. cm.
    ISBN 0-8010-1132-9 (cloth)
       1. High school graduates—Religious life. 2. Young adults—Religious
    life. 3. High school graduates—Conduct of life. 4. Young adults—Conduct of life. I. Title.
    BV4529.2.025 1997
    248.8'3—dc21   96-40857

Introduction

Who would have ever thought that you'd go from eating goldfish in Mrs. Stanislavski's kindergarten classroom to graduating from high school in thirteen short years?

"Excuse me," you say. "Did you say thirteen short years?"

Okay, okay, so maybe those years in the penitentiary, I mean school system, weren't so short, especially this last year . . . your senior year . . . the longest year of your life. I'm not sure if you've given it much thought, but don't you find it slightly suspicious that the number of years it takes to receive a diploma from grades K–12 correlates exactly with the number 13? Scary.

As a high school graduate, you probably won't have to worry too much about weird superstitions. Besides, you've got a lot more on your mind than that. You've just celebrated one of your most important accomplishments to date. By now, you've probably signed tons of yearbooks, writing down hilarious moments and cherished memories shared with your friends. There've been parties, all-night celebrations—lots of photos and video moments recorded. You've promised lifelong friendships and made summer plans. You are now ready to venture out and claim your piece of the planet.

Life after high school can be exciting and thrilling, marked by all kinds of positive changes and new experiences. You may be moving away to a university, taking on a new job, enrolling in a trade school, signing up for classes at the local junior college, or even joining the military. Whatever your plans in discovering your piece of the planet, I certainly hope God's best for you. Why? Because God has bigger and better plans than you or I can even hope for ourselves. And, in case no one has told you yet, taking your piece of the planet can be pretty scary stuff . . . especially if you bite off more than you can chew!

That's why I wrote this book.

Excuse Me! I'll Take My Piece of the Planet Now is not a detailed road map to tell you how to live your life. It's more of a guidebook, like the ones you'll buy if you ever go backpacking through Europe. It is designed to help you make good decisions in your travels throughout this life. It will tell you about the adventures of other young people, friends of mine, and how they are carving out their piece of the planet. It will point you in the right direction for the many choices you will face as well as help you steer clear of some of this planet's many hazards. Above all else, it will provide you the best direction from the finest road map available. That road map is God's Word, the Bible, written for your stay here on planet Earth.

After all, if you really want to be all that God has designed you to be, make sure that Jesus Christ is your travel companion on this planet. You see, your ultimate destination is heaven, and this planet is really not your home. Taking your piece of the planet means being all God has designed you to be here on earth while keeping your eyes on heaven. Like anyone else, you're not perfect. You'll make mistakes along the way. There'll be periods of time when you feel like you are lost. You'll be tempted to give up. That's when you'll want to scratch these words on a piece of paper and keep it in your pocket: ⟶

But one thing I do: Forgetting what is behind and straining toward what is ahead, I press on toward the goal to win the prize for which God has called me heavenward in Christ Jesus.

PHILIPPIANS
3:13–14

Taking your piece of the planet means pressing on toward the abundant life to which God has called you. There is no higher calling for your life. Don't just settle for a piece of this planet; press on . . . go for the prize—the ultimate prize in Christ Jesus.

EXCUSE ME!"

I'm Going to Be Who God Wants Me to Be.

1

BE AUTHENTIC

The Scene

Have you ever met a psychotic liar? Psychotic liars are only entertaining if you know they're lying. Since you know aliens have stolen their brains, all you have to do is sit back, nod, hum, tilt your head as if you're really interested, and enjoy the amazing "Made for TV" adventure stories they create. If you don't know they're lying, it's another matter; you may end up buying toxic waste dumps.

I had just finished speaking at a singles Bible study when I met my first psychotic liar. Jim Grindle, the singles pastor, and I had just sat down with our double-double-low-fat-hold-the-lemon-twist-decaf-espressos when a guy in his late thirties walked up and asked if he could join us. He said it was his first time attending the Bible study. He seemed like a nice guy. Nothing unusual. So I thought.

Like the bursting, staccato rattle of a semi-automatic machine gun, this guy unleashed his fiery assault. "Hey, remember all those pink-yellow-green neon colors back in the eighties . . . I invented those for the surf industry.

"I'm looking to start an international merchandise business for Christians only. It would only be for REAL Christians and I need someone to help with my marketing plan. Are you interested?"

I know as much about international marketing as I do Mandarin Chinese, but that didn't discourage this guy. He went on.

"I'm just glad my son is okay. Last week, his brother shot him in the head with a BB gun. That thing went right into his brain, but he's okay now.

"Yeah, I'm a millionaire. I've got a big mansion up on the hill . . . maybe we can have the Bible study up there and. . . ." *Zzzzzzzzzzzzz!*

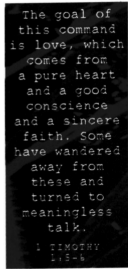

The goal of this command is love, which comes from a pure heart and a good conscience and a sincere faith. Some have wandered away from these and turned to meaningless talk.

1 TIMOTHY 1:5-6

The slice

Somehow I don't think this guy's mini-dramas were true. They weren't real. They weren't authentic. *He* wasn't authentic. Inauthenticity is one of the dangers you may face after leaving high school. It's an attitude some young people have that goes like this: *That part of my life is over. When I get away, I'm going to be someone completely different.*

If you're looking to make changes after high school, be sure to move in the direction of authenticity. Move towards who you are and away from role-playing. One of the dangers of new surroundings is pretending to be someone you're not. Some people grow up in stifling, oppressive homes where they are forced to be someone they're not.

They're pressured to be an imitation of their parents. In the search to find themselves, they completely reject everything about their former life. Including their faith. Don't reject your faith in favor of someone you're not. It's not necessary to lose your faith in order to find yourself. I've seen far too many students put enormous amounts of energy into trying to be someone they're not. Instead of accepting themselves for who God created them to be and discovering their identity in Christ, they're like a leopard trying to wash off his spots.

If you want to change, be yourself and make changes for the better. If you were a joking loudmouth in high school and you know that's not the real you, you can make a change for the better. Just because you were known as a party animal in high school, that doesn't mean you can never change from doing drugs and alcohol. If you're going to change, go for the genuine, authentic changes the Holy Spirit wants to bring about in your life. If you're confused about who you are, accept the confusion for what it is. Don't deny it, hide it, or pretend it doesn't exist. Admit your confusion and questions to God. Ask him for help. He can handle it. God wants to produce real, authentic changes in you. Authenticity is the only place to start.

Character is the one thing you can't hide. Though you may try to cover your spots or stripes, true character eventually comes out. Paul and Timothy faced deceitful Christians in the church whose true characters were anything but authentic. They were causing all sorts of controversies in the early church, so Paul told a young Timothy to tell these older guys to stop teaching false doctrines. Paul directed Timothy to let his motivations stem from an authentic character of love, a pure heart, a good conscience, and sincere faith. In essence he said, "Timothy, just be yourself. Handle this controversy with an authentic, godly character." Paul later says, "Some have rejected these and so have shipwrecked their faith." Do you want an authentic faith or a shipwrecked faith? Let people see the same person God sees. Be yourself. At all costs, strive to be authentic in all you say and do . . . even if you really do become a millionaire someday.

The Stand

How do you feel when someone is not being real with you? How can you be your authentic self and keep your faith in Christ alive after high school? In what ways are you tempted to be someone you're not? What are the risks involved in being yourself? What steps can you take to develop an attitude of authenticity in all you say and do?

2

GEN X GRUMBLING

The Scene

One of the charges leveled against Baby Busters, or Generation X, is that they have an unusually pessimistic outlook on life. You can pick up any magazine or newspaper today (probably written by a Baby Boomer) and read: *Baby Busters are angry. Ticked off. They're cynical. They hate Baby Boomers.* Generation X members have been called crybabies, pouters, and complainers. The younger generation is supposedly characterized by angst, anger, and alienation. The despairing lyrics of Nirvana, Pearl Jam, Toad the Wet Sprocket, Counting Crows, and Nine Inch Nails have led social critics of Generation X to write this generation off as a bunch of whiners.

What do you think? Me? I fall somewhere in the middle. I have a number of young friends who are angry, negative, pessimistic, and filled with excuses for why they are the way they are. They do have a very cynical view of life.

They're ticked off at parents who were too busy licking their wounds from divorce and failed relationships to pay attention to their children's needs for love and attention. For some of my college-age friends, McDonald's and 7-Eleven are the only employment opportunities they see. No, the future is not something they are real excited about. Until things change, they've chosen to furrow their brows and brood about their lives.

On the other hand, I also know dozens of young people who aren't anything at all like the pessimistic, anger-filled *Newsweek* and *Time* magazine stereotypes. They are positive people, and fun to be around. Sure, they have problems like anyone else, but they have chosen not to conform to the pessimistic attitudes commonly associated with their generation. They're not whiners, complainers, or crybabies. They are young people who have a clear sense that God is a lot bigger than the temporary problems of their generation. Instead of fearing the future, they are thankful for how God has demonstrated his faithfulness in their lives. Thankfulness, not cynicism, seems to be their attitude of choice. They live with an attitude of gratitude.

Therefore, since we are receiving a kingdom that cannot be shaken, let us be thankful, and so worship God acceptably with reverence and awe, for our God is a consuming fire.

HEBREWS 12:28-29

The slice

What is your attitude of choice? What matters most is not what critics say or what's happening in our society around you, but what's happening inside you. What matters most is your attitude. What matters most is whether you choose to be thankful or not.

The fastest cure for pessimism is a thankful heart. A thankful heart chooses to focus on what God has faithfully done in the past. A thankful heart rests in God's presence in the present. And a thankful heart trusts in God's unchanging promises for the future. Being thankful for God's faithfulness puts your present problems and pains in perspective. You can freeze the icy hold of cynicism by standing next to the warm blaze of God's consuming fire.

If you're angry about your family life or confused about the future, being thankful doesn't mean you have to deny those feelings. Being thankful means that you are making a deliberate choice to center your attention on God and not your circumstances. Being thankful doesn't mean that you'll never have problems or experience pain. Choosing to be thankful gives you an incredibly useful tool for dealing with problems and pain. It's a wonderful alternative to bitterness and pessimism. Thankfulness burns cynicism away.

The writer of Hebrews gives you a strong reason to be thankful today: in Jesus Christ, you are receiving a kingdom that cannot be shaken. That doesn't mean that someday, somewhere in heaven, you'll hopefully be happy. The kingdom of God that can't be shaken is God's present kingdom here on earth today and in the future (remember that English class I-N-G present participle stuff?). You are receiving God's kingdom now. The kingdom of God is in process right now. In your life. Jesus wants to live his kingdom through you.

So what's your response? What does Hebrews say? *Be thankful.* What do you have to be thankful for today? Despite how awful your situation may be, what will cynicism, anger, and pessimism do to change it? How are your attitudes related to the way you deal with struggles?

What else does Hebrews say? *Let us so worship God acceptably with reverence and awe.* Instead of brewing bitterness, many of my college-age friends choose to rivet their attention on God with reverence and awe. They have chosen to live in awe of God. They have chosen to worship instead of whining and worrying. Living in thankfulness, worship, reverence, and awe has transformed their lives like nothing else. The social critics would be amazed.

The Stand

Take a piece of paper and write down at least ten things you are thankful for. Do that every time you're feeling down. Carry your list in your purse or pocket. Being thankful will change your perspective. It will change your life!

3

SURF TUNES

The Scene

It was the first big winter swell to hit the North Shore during the 1994/95 season. On a quiet Sunday morning of our Hawaiian Christmas vacation, I woke up early, left our beach house, and headed to check out the waves. Driving up the coast I noticed the churning, foaming, white water of the outer coral reefs. As the road curved toward the North Shore, the strong onshore wind from the eastern windward side of the island became an offshore wind, creating lacy veils over the thick crests of each powerful, thundering, monstrous wave, kind of like a weird combination of the *Bride of Frankenstein* and *Victory at Sea*.

I pulled into the parking lot of Sunset Beach. A thick blanket of white foam covered the water's turbulent surface. Like a relentless, advancing column of storm troopers, set after set of massive waves launched an all-out assault on the beach. The waves were triple-overhead, Hawaiian size (that means a ten-foot California wave, measured by the front, is a twenty-foot Hawaiian wave, measured by the back). Misty clouds of salt spray floated through the air. The offshore breezes smoothed the face of each wave, making the drop-in possible for the few brave surfers who dared to venture out.

After Sunset Beach, I headed down to the world famous Pipe-line. Known for its dangerous coral reef, Pipeline's power has paralyzed and killed plenty of surfers, thus earning its reputation as one of the most respected, awesome waves in the world. As the incoming waves triggered depth-charge-like explosions, I could almost feel the beach shake underneath my feet from the ocean's raw power.

The swells began to slowly break on the outermost, third reef. Out of an aggressive pack of over fifty surfers, many wearing helmets, one surfer caught the wave on the second reef and began a fast, bumpy descent toward the first reef. At that point, the locomotive force of the ocean swell jacked up the incoming wave twenty to twenty-five feet high as the surfer made a long, sweeping bottom turn.

Lining up for a tube tall enough to drive a semi-truck through, the surfer disappeared into the enormous tube for one, two, three, four, five seconds. Then, blasting out a spitting explosion of water like a cannon emptying its ammunition, the wave expelled its human contents. With a quick turn off the wave, the surfer slid to his stomach and paddled out for the next set. Screams and hollers went up from the crowd on the beach. Were they applauding the surfer . . . or God's amazing creation?

The slice

The Bible says that even the seas, every ocean in the world, have lifted their voices to God. Even the massive twenty-foot Pipeline surf is a thundering chorus of creation, praising God for his power. If creation praises the work of its Creator, what should be our response to God? Standing in front of a killer twenty-five-foot wave

> The seas have lifted up, O Lord, the seas have lifted up their voice; the seas have lifted up their pounding waves. Mightier than the thunder of the great waters, mightier than the breakers of the sea—the Lord on high is mighty.
>
> PSALM 93:3-4

can make you feel pretty small. And powerless. And scared. Waves like that create a healthy respect and desire to live. As a follower of Jesus Christ, you have the privilege of praising God, the creator of the universe. You can praise the one who is mightier than the waves of the sea. Praising God is one of the best ways you can show your love and devotion to him. Developing a daily attitude of praise lifts you out of the subtle, negative attitudes that can dampen your heart for God.

Giving your praise to God is so simple, but it's often replaced by a quick-fix-get-something-from-God shopping list of requests and demands. Instead of being a "getter" from God, why not be a praise-giver? Developing an attitude of praise will get your eyes off your immediate problems and circumstances by placing your attention on God's unlimited source of power, strength, and provision. In Christ Jesus, God promises to richly meet all your needs. Instead of whipping out a daily checklist, why don't you develop a list of praises for how you see God at work in the world around you? Being a praise-giver is a sure way to see God's power at work.

The Stand

Giving praise to God transforms the way you look at life. Spend some time wandering through the Book of Psalms. It's filled with praise and honor to God. Read one psalm every day this week. Then create your own psalm by writing down everything you want to praise God for.

4

WHAT'S YOUR MAJOR?

The Scene

If you're heading to college after graduation, you have the daunting task of declaring an academic major. A specialty. That's a task some students have already figured out. *I'm going to be a business major. I'm declaring pre-med. I'm going to major in English.* Don't fear when you see these self-assured peers not stressed or worried about declaring a major. Most of them knew what field they were going to study by the time they were four years old. Most of us are not like them and that's okay.

Since the average college student changes his or her major four to six times, don't worry about declaring a major the first day you step foot on campus. In case anyone hasn't told you yet, you have at least two years of General Ed classes to take before you need to declare a major. If someone asks you your major and you feel embarrassed that you have no clue about what you want to study, here are some carefully selected, socially acceptable answers. Just say,

➥ *"Communications" (it sounds really good, but no one's really sure what communications majors study; sounds like you'll be a newscaster).*

➥ *"Humanities" (where could you possibly go wrong studying the human race? It's also boring enough to end the conversation).*

➥ *"Advanced Speleological Symmetry" (if your questioners look confused at this answer, that's good; ask them the average drip rate of a stalactite onto a stalagmite).*

Too many people get worked up over what they're going to major in. Declaring a major is not the most important task you face in this life. You will eventually choose a major you'll probably enjoy. Just don't forget to choose the most important major of all: a major in life.

The slice

Don't get me wrong here. You may be freaking out about picking a major and I make it sound like no big deal. Yes, selecting a major is a big deal. But it's not a BIG, BIG deal. It's not a HUGE deal or a HUMONGOUS deal; it's just a big deal, with a little "b." Too many freshmen and sophomores make it a Big deal (with a Big B) and they end up missing the most important major of all. Instead of majoring in life, some students choose to merely learn about Andizhan economic theory, zygomatic facial bones, or primitive protozoans.

Majoring in life begins with an intentional attitude to become a lifelong learner. A recent article in the *Los Angeles Times* cited the increase in double, triple, and even quadruple majors in California colleges and universities. The article states that students with double or triple majors are more marketable after college, especially in a competitive job market. Having more than one major doesn't make you a lifelong learner. Sure, a triple major may increase your chances of getting a job, but by the time you graduate, you may be ready to retire.

College is a wonderful place to become a lifelong learner, and it starts with an attitude of keeping your relationship with God alive throughout your college years. Be a lifelong learner of God. A disciple. That's what disciple means . . . a learner. Don't let books or theories or majors or final exams keep you from seeing the bigger picture. The BIG, BIG picture.

When you get to college, don't hibernate your faith like a fat, old bear asleep in a smelly, damp cave. Incubate your faith with new ideas. Integrate your faith with your classes. Incorporate your commitment to Christ in the new relationships you make. Being a learner is not parroting the right answer handed down from an all-knowing, sanctimonious, revered professor. It's developing that uncanny, fearless attitude of asking that one question everyone else is scared to death to ask (but hoping someone like you will ask).

King Solomon is known as being the wisest, smartest, most intelligent man in the whole world. He also had lots of bucks, stuff, and women. But the one thing that stands out about Solomon is that he was a lifelong learner. The Book of Ecclesiastes is his personal journal, his reflections about what is most important in life. After having everything a person could ever wish or desire, Solomon concluded that the most important thing in this life, the one really BIG thing to keep learning all your life, is how to fear God and keep his commandments. That's what matters most.

> Be warned, my son, of anything in addition to them. Of making many books there is no end, and much study wearies the body. Now all has been heard; here is the conclusion of the matter: Fear God and keep his commandments, for this is the whole duty of man.
>
> ECCLESIASTES 12:12-13

Developing an attitude of being a lifelong learner begins with fearing God and keeping his commandments. That's real success. Don't trade God for books. Or a major. Be like Solomon. Be wise. Be a lifelong learner by fearing God and honoring him by keeping his commands. Take time to get your face out of the books and keep discovering what's really most important in life. It'll take you a lifetime.

The Stand

What new areas of your faith do you want to explore? What can you do to develop an attitude of being a lifelong learner? If you were to explain to someone what it means to be a lifelong learner, what would you tell them? Write down three of the most important qualities or attitudes of a lifelong learner. Now write a specific way you'd like to integrate each one of these qualities into your life. What have you learned so far?

EXCUSE ME!'

Are You My Friend or What?

5

FRIENDS FOR LIFE?

The Scene

My wife, Krista, and I recently went to a bagel shop for breakfast. As we ordered our cinnamon bagels, cream cheese, and steaming cups of coffee, we met a college student who used to be active in our youth ministry. The girl's name was Kim. In high school, she hung out with a fun gang of friends. Most of them had never gone to church before, but as a group, they went on trip after trip with our outreach ministry.

Kim was now attending the local junior college and we asked her if she still hung out with the old gang. In an instant, she dropped her smile.

"No," she said. "None of us spend any time together. The gang's no longer a gang. We've all kind of gone our separate ways."

We talked to Kim a little bit more and finally said goodbye. Afterwards, Krista and I wondered how suddenly friendships change after high school. In our estimation, Kim didn't seem to be the fun, friendly, bubbly high school girl we used to know. It was obvious by the tone of her voice and the look on her face that Kim longed for the meaningful, fun friendships she used to have in high school.

We spent some time talking about Kim and her crazy group of friends. "I wonder how they're doing," I thought out loud to Krista. Despite all the hilarious times, wild adventures, fun ski trips, and heart-to-heart cabin talks, there was nothing any of us could have done to stop Kim's friendships from changing. Yes, it was sad. A lot of teenagers think that their junior and senior high friends will be friends for life. But sometimes "friends for life" don't last that long. Sometimes the gang is no longer a gang.

The slice

I hope the friendships you developed in high school will be some of your closest friends for life. Those special friendships are worth keeping. They are worth your continued effort and investment to develop. Unfortunately, as Kim experienced, the special high school friendships that are supposed to last a lifetime often don't last a year or two after graduation day.

> A man of many companions may come to ruin, but there is a friend who sticks closer than a brother.
>
> PROVERBS 18:24

In high school, many friends pledge to be friends for life. Senior photos are exchanged. Special songs are shared. Prom dates are carefully planned together. Long letters and hours hanging on the phone help cement friendships designed to last forever. Then something weird happens. That something weird is graduation day. For some friendships—not all, happily—graduation day changes everything. Graduation changes friendships.

I can remember what some people wrote in my senior yearbook. "Dude, we'll be radical friends forever. See ya at the beach. Steve." "Joey, stay cool. You'll always be my friend. Julie." I haven't seen Steve or Julie in twelve years. Life after graduation changed our friendships. Steve and Julie changed. I changed.

Most people won't tell you the types of changes to expect after high school. Friendships are an area you can expect to change. You'll see some friends desert God as if they never knew him at all. Some of your friends' priorities and lifestyles will change radically. Some may appear on your doorstep at one A.M. with purple hair and a pierced belly button while chanting Tibetan nursery rhymes. Other friends will go wacko, and you'll read about them in the newspaper. A few friends will even say to you, "You've changed." You have. And so have they. Graduation changes everyone. Some for better. Others for worse.

The one friendship you can expect to keep after high school is your friendship with Jesus. He promises to be your friend for life. Though you will undoubtedly experience changes in your friendship with him, the changes Jesus wants you to experience are positive, life-giving changes.

Jesus promises to stick closer to you than a brother. He pledges to never leave you or forsake you. He's committed to help you through the changes you experience after high school. Jesus will always be your Lord and friend. For life.

The Stand

Some of your friendships will change after high school. Some won't. It depends on you and your friends. The best investment you can make for the friends you want to keep for life is to talk about how your friendships might be different after high school. Meet with your close friends and develop action steps to keep your friendships alive. Ask yourselves, what do you need to do to keep Jesus at the center of your friendships? How can you be his friend for life?

FEELING LONELY AFTER HIGH SCHOOL

The Scene

Have you ever bawled into a bowl of cereal? I did a lot of times as a kid, but the time I least expected to was when I was a college student. My sophomore year of college had just begun and I was attending school in northern California. My freshman year had gone just okay. I liked school but wasn't thrilled about it. College wasn't anything like high school. In high school, I had a lot of friends and an endless amount of things to do. During my freshman year of college, I hadn't made very many friends. Of the friends I did have, none were really close friends. At that time, none of my college friends were like my high school friends.

It was dinnertime and I headed to the school cafeteria for another exquisite experience in fine collegiate *haute cuisine* (English translation: dogfood). Gravy Train was out of the question, the cafeteria was out of Kibbles 'n'

Bits, and since I had Alpo the night before, I settled for a bowl of granola. It's hard to mess up oats and raisins.

Walking carefully with cereal in hand, I surveyed the cafeteria for someone I knew, someone to sit with and eat my cereal. Making my way around the tables with a wandering, searching gaze, I couldn't find anyone I knew, so I sat down. Alone with my cereal. Alone with myself. Alone.

After a few minutes of sitting by myself, I began to think about all the friends I had in high school and how I now had no one to even sit with for dinner. I thought to myself, "This sucks. Why am I feeling this way? Why am I feeling so lonely?"

That's when tears began to run down my face. For the first time in my life, I was crying tears of loneliness. I hated having dinner by myself. I hated eating stupid cereal for dinner. I hated not having any good friends at college. I hated feeling lonely. I hated being alone.

The slice

There's no feeling like loneliness to crush your spirit. Loneliness is that empty, isolated feeling I believe many young people experience after they graduate from high school. Loneliness catches a lot of young people by surprise. It's often unexpected because if you were used to making friends in high school, your new university surroundings can be a cold, unfriendly environment you hadn't anticipated. When I went to college, I expected to meet friends right away because that's supposed to happen in college. Your parents tell you that these will be the best years of your life. You hear comments like, "In college, you'll make the best friends you've ever had!" Right? All I can say is, "Maybe."

At the same time, the opposite can also be true. Perhaps you experienced a lot of loneliness in high school and now that you've

> The righteous cry out, and the LORD hears them; he delivers them from all their troubles. The LORD is close to the brokenhearted and saves those who are crushed in spirit. A righteous man may have many troubles, but the Lord delivers him from them all.
>
> PSALM
> 34:17-19

graduated, you're making more friends than you've ever had before. Maybe you're already starting your career and you've made a lot of friends at work. You could be in college right now and making friends hasn't been a problem. If so, I hope that's true. I hope loneliness hasn't been a problem for you.

But if you find your tears making your cereal soggy, I want you to know it's okay to feel lonely after high school. Graduation was probably an incredible high and a dramatic relief for you. It was one of the turning points in your life, marking the end of your high school years. The wonderful feelings of celebration and success you felt can also be accompanied by uncertain, scary feelings of change and transition. Loneliness is a gross feeling that often comes after graduation. In that, you're not alone.

I know it sounds like something learned in a third grade Sunday school class, but what really did comfort me when I felt lonely in college was knowing that God was with me. Knowing that Jesus promised to be my friend gave me a strong sense of security when I felt insecure about not having any close friends. Jesus gave me the courage to go out and make new friends.

God promises to be with you when you're brokenhearted. He understands your deep, gnawing feelings of loneliness. He wants to deliver you from your troubles and help you through the painful process of loneliness. Accepting God's friendship can give you his friendship for eternity. Knowing that God is your friend may not dissolve all your feelings of loneliness. God's friendship won't poof loneliness away like pixie dust, but it will definitely provide his presence and support. Give your loneliness to God. Don't be afraid to ask him for the friends you need. Don't be afraid to ask for his friendship either. Loneliness isn't worth a soggy bowl of cereal.

The Stand

Taking a giant step to leap out of loneliness usually happens by forcing yourself to make new friends or making the effort to keep in touch with your old friends. Either way, it's going to require some effort on your part. Take some time to examine why you're feeling lonely. Whom could you talk to? How do you think God wants you to deal with your loneliness? What are some positive things you could do to deal with the loneliness?

7

KILLER EXPECTATIONS

The Scene

"Your honor, I don't have the money to pay this parking ticket. It was my very first time at the San Francisco airport and I was just helping a friend who had to fly back to Iowa. I even had to borrow a car to get her there. I didn't see any 'No Parking' signs."

"Very well," the judge said, peering over his glasses. "Case dismissed."

A warm wave of relief rushed over me as I rejoiced in not having to pay the 150-dollar parking fine. What had started as a simple friendship was now a twisted mess of parking tickets, long letters begging me to write, suicide threats, and unexpected gifts in the mail. *If I had only known then what I know now!*

I'm going to chop this very long story into a mini-docudrama about how killer, unrealistic expectations can destroy a friendship. I first met Diane at church when I was a freshman in college. She was a friendly, heavyset girl who had just moved out from Iowa a month earlier. After working as a live-in baby-sitter for a month, she was fired. The youth pastor and his wife took her in while she looked for a new job. Since I was new to the area and she was too, I figured she might enjoy spending a day sight-seeing in San Francisco. I didn't think much of it. I was just trying to be friendly. Call me naive, dumb, or just a plain idiot . . . I was all of those things.

After one day of sight-seeing, Diane stuck to me like a nail in an unsuspecting steel-belted radial tire. There were "surprise" visits at my campus. She called me every day just to talk. I received letters in the mail. She just happened to show up on the jogging trail she knew I ran every day. She asked me why I didn't call her more. After only two weeks of knowing her, Diane told me that she was falling in love with me. *Ga-ga-ga-wha-wha-WHAT!!??*

The slice

Love must be sincere. Hate what is evil; cling to what is good. Be devoted to one another in brotherly love. Honor one another above your-selves.

ROMANS
12:9-10

After I told Diane I just wanted to be her friend, her pursuit continued. She was a lonely, hurting girl whose needs and expectations for our friendship far exceeded anything I could give. A month later, Diane finally went back to Iowa. After the "take-me-to-the-airport-get-a-parking-ticket-borrow-another-car-defend-myself-in-court" scene, I began to get collect calls from Iowa. On Christmas vacation, she relentlessly called me at all hours. Though she "had no money," I received an expensive Christmas present of two sweaters, a scarf, and a large box of stationery (hint, hint) to use to write to her. "This is ridiculous," I told myself. "She's got to stop calling me." The next time Diane called, I asked her not to call me anymore. She didn't listen to me.

Diane called back, but this time she called to tell me that she had just swallowed a whole bottle of sleeping pills and that an ambulance was on the way to take her to the hospital. My response was, "I'm very sorry to hear that, but I don't know how to help you, Diane." Not only could I not meet her killer expectations, our friendship had become so convoluted that I wasn't able to help her when she needed help the most.

Have you ever had a friend with killer expectations? Do you feel like you're being manipulated to give more than you can in a friendship? Or are you a person who puts a lot of pressure on your friend to be a better friend? Do you use guilt trips and killer expectations on your friends? Don't be fooled by a manipulative friend. What they say sounds good: "I don't understand why nobody loves me . . . I love everybody." What they're really saying is what my pastor Denny Bellesi jokingly says, "I AM THE ALL-CONSUMING BLACK HOLE OF THE UNIVERSE AND I WILL DO ANYTHING TO SUCK YOU INTO MY RAGING VORTEX."

Nothing will destroy a friendship quicker than unrealistic expectations. Killer expectations suffocate friendships because stringent, demanding expectations don't allow the other person room to breathe. Killer expectations make friendships lopsided, tipping the balance of how friendships are designed to work. No one can meet all of our needs for friendship, love, and acceptance. If you have used unreasonable demands, guilt, and various forms of manipulation (like Diane) to gain friends, it will ultimately push others away from you.

Paul said that love must be sincere. That includes friendships. A sincere friendship is characterized by realistic expectations and not unreal demands inflicted upon one person. Friends ought to be devoted to one another, but only if there is freedom in the relationship. Using guilt or scare tactics to coerce a friend does not honor anyone. Don't depend on one person to meet all your needs. You'll only hurt yourself. And the other person.

Watch out for killer expectations . . . honor your friends before yourself.

The Stand

What are your friendships like? Balanced and mutual? Or suspicious and questionable? Use the "Killer Expectation Checklist" to evaluate your friends.

Do they . . .

❏ Use manipulative behavior?

❏ Make unrealistic demands on your time?

❏ Make threats?

❏ Have a victim mentality?

❏ Use attention-getting behavior?

❏ Pout and whine a lot?

❏ Use guilt trips?

❏ Use silence as a weapon?

❏ Say things like, "If you were really my friend..."

❏ Only want to be with you?

How are sincere love, devotion, and honor demonstrated in your friendships?

IN SEARCH OF
NEW FRIENDS

The Scene

Krista graduated from high school a semester early so she could go to Saddleback Junior College to play on the women's tennis team. In high school, she was shy and never had all the friends she wished she had. Maybe, she thought, going to college early would give her a chance at making new friends.

On the tennis team, she quickly got to know her new teammates. Her team traveled all over California and Hawaii for tournaments. She soon discovered that her tennis partners were, for the most part, nice girls, but they did have a bit of a wild streak. Since Krista was a Christian and God was the top priority in her life, she quickly found out that her lifestyle was very different than that of some of the girls on her team. Some of her teammates liked to party, drink, and sleep around.

Though Krista got along with her teammates, they weren't exactly the kind of friends she had in mind. She wanted friends who wouldn't pressure her to be or do anything she didn't want to. She wanted intimate, close friends with whom she could travel and have fun, friends who didn't need drugs or alcohol as a substitute for pleasure. She also desired friends who could encourage her in her relationship with God and with whom she could share the most important person in her life.

Krista could have taken the easy way and started to party with her tennis teammates, but she knew that if she did, she wouldn't be true to God or to herself. She didn't want friends who just liked her because she partied with them. So, instead of becoming like her tennis teammates, she began to pray for new friends. Even though she was lonely, she wasn't willing to sacrifice her friendship with Jesus for just any type of new friends. I'm glad she didn't. If she did, I probably would have never met my future wife.

The slice

Therefore, my brothers, you whom I love and long for, my joy and crown, that is how you should stand firm in the Lord, dear friends!

PHILIPPIANS 4:1

Standing firm in Christ is the true secret to friendship with God. Trading friendship with God for friends who couldn't care less about who God is or what he thinks is like choosing to serve a tennis ball into the net. You double fault by backhanding God and picking the wrong kind of teammates. Finding new friends doesn't have to come at the expense of losing your relationship with God. As a loving Father who knows your every need, God wants you to have significant, meaningful relationships with other people. If you are searching for new friends, have you considered talking to God about your needs?

After a few months of regular prayer (and refusing to give in to her teammates' lifestyle), Krista began to see answers to her prayer for friends. God didn't answer her prayers immediately by dropping a hundred new friends on her doorstep, but one by one, Krista began meeting people she enjoyed spending time with. She became involved in a large music ministry production and started attending a church with a lot of young people. As one thing led to another, one night Krista invited a bunch of people over to her house to go swimming. Before she realized what had happened, over twenty people were running around the pool, raiding the refrigerator, watching TV, and having a blast. From that one night, Krista's home became a regular hangout for the next five years. Incidentally, since we had all become a large gang of friends, it took me at least two years to get a date with Krista. She was afraid that dating "one of the gang" would mess up all her other friendships.

I sincerely believe God honored Krista's prayer for new friends because Krista honored her friendship with God. Instead of conforming to those around her, Krista chose to stand firm in the Lord. Her first love and longing was for God, not friends. Even though she was lonely at times, her friendship with God got her through the difficult process of finding new friends.

If you're looking for new friends, take a long-term look at your relationship with God and ask yourself what ultimately matters most. Take steps to find positive, healthy friendships with people who will accept you for who you are. Get involved with a college ministry. Find a place where other young people your age are serving others in the name of Christ. Don't just try to find any friend. Find a friend who will strengthen your friendship with God. That's the kind of friend worth praying for.

The Stand

Great friends are a wonderful gift from the Lord. When it comes to finding new friends, don't settle for second best. Look for friends who will influence your growth in the things of God and friends you can draw into his kingdom. Ask God to give you wisdom in finding and choosing new friends. Pray for what is specifically on your heart about wanting friends. Write down the top five qualities you look for in a friend. What are the top five qualities you don't want in a friend? What are some positive steps you can take this week to find new friends? What kinds of obstacles might you face? Are you willing to make your friendship with God your first priority?

EXCUSE ME!

for freaking Out!

FEARING THE END ZONE

The Scene

Each Friday in the *Los Angeles Times* there's an interesting section I always try to read. It's called "OC High: Student News and Views." OC High contains articles, thoughts, and interviews from Southern California high school students on a wide variety of topics. Last spring, an article called "The End Zone" caught my attention. The article quoted a number of graduating seniors who stated the fears they face about the so-called beginning of "adult life," and going to work or college. See if their statements catch your attention like they did mine:

"That my parents will come and visit me at college" (Sara, seventeen).

"I'm afraid I won't be able to hack it" (Sharon, seventeen).

"Trying to support myself" (Frank, eighteen).

"I'm most afraid of partying too much and flunking out, as well as the fact that I won't have my parents to fall back on" (David, seventeen).

"Failure. It's frightening when people are expecting you to succeed" (Misty, eighteen).

"Going away, not knowing anyone, no home cooking, and no easy money" (William, seventeen).

"Knowing anything and everything I do is up to me. There will be no assistance and guidelines to follow; you're just a number to them; they don't wait for you. You get it or you don't" (Rodney, eighteen).

"That the classes will be really hard" (Trisha, seventeen).

"I fear being alone at college" (Lisa, eighteen).

"Not making it" (Carrol, eighteen).

"Getting a really psychotic roommate" (Lindsey, seventeen).

The slice

Psychotic roommates. Loneliness. Financial struggles. Leaving family and friends behind. Flunking out. Failure. Those are all very real and valid fears as you face the end zone of high school and head into the twilight zone of life after graduation. If you are fearing the end zone of high school, know you're not alone. For every one student who's willing to admit that they're scared of life after high school, I bet there's another twenty who're feeling the same thing.

The good news of the gospel is that you don't have to face your fears alone. Though you may feel stranded and scared, Jesus Christ is standing right next to you waiting to strengthen you with his

> But now, this is what the LORD says — he who created you, O Jacob, he who formed you, O Israel: "Fear not, for I have redeemed you; I have summoned you by name; you are mine. When you pass through the waters, I will be with you; and when you pass through the rivers, they will not sweep over you. When you walk through the fire, you will not be burned; the flames will not set you ablaze."
>
> ISAIAH 43:1-2

presence as you put your trust in him. The very God who created you and loves you says, "You don't have to be frozen by your fears. I am with you. I have called you by name. You are mine." Aren't those great words?

Whether you're wondering if you're going to get a psycho roommate or if you're going to find the right job with the right pay so you can support yourself, have you stopped to consider that God is with you? God has called you by name. You are God's. You are intimately known and loved by your heavenly Father. He promises to be with you when you're flooded by fears. He promises to throw you a life preserver when you feel like you're getting swept downriver by pressures and problems. He promises you won't get torched into a crispy-critter, smokin' piece of burnt toast when you face fiery trials and temptations.

Through every problem, every fear, every worry . . . God is with you. You are his. Facing the end zone of high school is a new beginning to see God at work in wonderful new ways in your life. You are empowered by the living God. There is no fear too big, too impossible, too wild for him to handle. It doesn't matter what other high school students' fears are; you can give your fears to God today. You can have his peace today. You don't have to fear not making it. With God, you will make it.

The Stand

What fears are you facing about life after high school? What scares you about the future? The first step to finding God's peace is handing your fears to him. Make the deliberate choice to trade your fears for his peace. Write down the fears you are facing today. Ask God to replace your fears with his peace. Ask him to help you to trust him even when it doesn't make sense. Pray for God's direction in all the plans, decisions, and upcoming events in your future.

TOP TEN

pets for dorm room
PROTECTION

So, you're kind of scared about your new college environment. You've looked around town and you're wondering if your new surroundings are safe. Here are ten easy ways to calm your fears. Instead of buying those dangerous personal security devices like Mace or four-hundred-thousand-volt Tazer guns, get one of these animals to meet all your security needs.

1. **SUMATRAN TIGER.** The growl alone will keep strangers from even opening the door.

2. **BOA CONSTRICTOR.** Quiet. Stealthy. Able to land on people from your bookshelf. No evidence once swallowed. Don't have to feed for months.

3. **AFRICAN SCORPION.** Quick. Comes in low for the attack. Deadly within minutes. One sting is all it takes.

4. **CONGO RIVER PIRANHAS.** Your intruder may have to fall into your fish tank, but once he does, he ain't coming out.

5. **KOMODO DRAGON.** The sign on the door is enough to warn any attacker about your pet lizard. It just doesn't say it's a seven-foot-long, flesh-eating monster.

6. **TWIN VULTURES.** They'll fly above outside your dorm room, so no one will even attempt to enter. It'll give 'em the creeps.

7. **AFRICAN KILLER BEES.** Any hostile invader will quickly get the point. About a million of 'em.

8. **CONGO RIVER CROCODILE.** Easily hides under your bed. Promises to clean up the mess once finished with dinner.

9. **MALARIA-CARRYING MOSQUITO.** All you need is one. A prolonged, slow, feverish death.

10. **DOBERMAN PINSCHER.** These suckers have always been mean. Buy twin spiked collars (one for you, one for the dog) and go for a walk around campus. No one will bother you. I guarantee it.

10

GETTING STUCK

The Scene

On the hot, dry summer day of July 6, 1994, a small forest fire in the Glenwood Springs area of the Colorado Rocky Mountains erupted into an explosive, furious firestorm. Similar to the thousands of small forest fires put out every year by Colorado firefighters, no one imagined the slow, creeping blaze approaching Stone King Mountain would be any different. Nobody anticipated an entire mountainside spontaneously combusting into a hurricane of flames. They were wrong. Dead wrong.

Initially ordered to clear helicopter landing sites, a team of forty-nine firefighters gathered on Stone King Mountain to take a stand against the approaching blaze. Pushed by hot, high winds, the South Canyon fire began to consume the extremely dry oak- and pinion-covered base of Stone King Mountain. As the fire consumed more and more fuel, climbing higher and higher, the fire crews were alerted and told to retreat to the ridgeline for helicopter evacuation. Weighted down by heavy axes, gallons of water, bulky clothing, chain saws, and backpacks, the firefighters began a slow, grueling march up the mountainside.

Without warning, in a matter of seconds, the South Canyon fire exploded up Stone King Mountain. From a small, seemingly harmless blaze, the forest fire transformed itself into a raging, ravenous beast. Now pursued by three-hundred-foot flames, the firefighters dropped everything and struggled to race up the mountain. Like a twisting, billowing, angry tornado of fire, the fiery monster consumed the entire mountainside. There was no place to run for safety. By the day's end, fourteen firefighters were confirmed dead.

The Slice

That tragic story reminds me of the countless conversations I've had with many young friends after they've graduated from high school. Like the fourteen firefighters who were burned to death by the Stone King Mountain firestorm, nearly every graduate feels stuck after high school. If not one way, then another. *Stuck by problems. Consumed by guilt. Trapped by a fiery wall of confusing feelings.*

It's not too difficult to get stuck

> For we know that our old self was crucified with him so that the body of sin might be done away with, that we should no longer be slaves to sin — because anyone who has died has been freed from sin. Now if we died with Christ, we believe that we will also live with him.
>
> ROMANS
> 6:6-8

after high school. For the first time in your life, you may not have the support of your family like you're used to. You could get stuck in your relationship with God. You may not be as excited about God as you once were. Now, God's more like an old girlfriend or boyfriend you occasionally greet in the hall. Unaware of the dangers of credit and debt, you may ring up a number of large bills you have no ability to pay. You could get stuck in a dead-end, abusive relationship, but since you're lonely, you hang on, hoping things will change. Declaring a certain major just because that's what your father studied is an almost sure way of getting stuck. How about that dilapidated, prehistoric piece of motored rust you're driving? You could get stuck just about anywhere driving that thing!

Getting stuck can make you feel like you're in an uphill race against a consuming fire. Getting stuck will make you feel trapped. Lonely. Paralyzed. Without hope. Getting stuck stinks. If you're ever going to get unstuck, you've got to be willing to fight fire with fire.

You don't have to be a slave to "stuck." If you're a Christian, you are no longer a slave to sin. You are not a slave to the habits, problems, and circumstances that get you stuck. Jesus Christ has set you free from the power of sin and death in your life. Those negative attitudes, destructive behavior patterns, temptations, and inner conflicts can be extinguished by the power of God in your life. Though getting stuck makes you feel pressured, powerless, and far from God, you can have hope because you are alive in Christ. Jesus will protect you from being consumed. He will keep you from getting torched. He will get you to the other side of the mountain.

The Stand

So how do you take steps to get unstuck? *First,* identify the problem. Is it an actual problem? Is it a worry? A fear? *Second,* write down three to five desired outcomes to your problem (how you'd like things to be different). *Third,* develop action steps, things you can do to solve your problems based on your desired outcomes. *Fourth*, meet with someone you trust who can help you get unstuck. Show them your game plan for getting unstuck. Ask for advice. Ask them to hold you accountable to stick to your commitment. Take these four steps and ask God to give you his strength to get unstuck.

1. Identify the problem

2. Write three to five desired outcomes

3. Develop action steps

4. Ask for accountability

11

FINDING
FREEDOM OVER FEAR

The Scene

Looking around the deserted park, I spied a lonely park bench. I sat down, took a deep breath, and inhaled the warm, late September air. Ah, Spain! I was in Valencia to study for my Spanish major. The beautiful park, full of quiet paths, whispering fountains, and colorful flowers, was empty because of the daily three-hour siesta. Little did I know that in Valencia, the third largest city in Spain, the only people who hung out in this park during the siesta were the fools and the robbers.

"Tienes cigarillo?" asked a young, tall, dark-skinned gypsy man who had quickly approached me. He was dirty, unshowered, and missing half of one of his front teeth. I gave a short, impersonal reply: "No fumo" (I don't smoke).

In a split second, a companion of his appeared, sat down next to me on the bench, picked up my knapsack, and began to rifle through it.

"Hey, what you are doing?" I yelled, grabbing at my knapsack. Not a good move. I suddenly felt pressure against my stomach. Reflecting the sun's glistening rays, a sleek, sharp, six-inch switchblade was being firmly held against my lower abdomen. Death, or at least serious injury, seemed to be a quick jab of the wrist away. I gasped and looked up, only to discover a second silvery switchblade held two inches from my heart. Surges of pumping adrenaline pulsated through my body. I remained motionless, not knowing what to do. Scream for help? *Nah.* Give 'em a Mel Gibson headbutt? *I don't think I feel like being a hero today.*

Frozen in fear and uncertainty of what might happen to me, I silently screamed to the Lord in desperation. *God. Help me. Don't let these guys stab me. Please, Jesus, you've got to protect me. You have to. Help!*

The slice

After almost being skewered like a Spanish bull, for the next three months I was in Spain I walked the streets of Valencia in terrible fear of getting held up again. My knife-packing thieves got away with plenty—one American dollar and a Casio watch. I received something undesirable in return, something I didn't ask for and had no way to return: fear. Most of the time I'd walk to and from class with my buddy, Dave. But whenever I was alone, it didn't matter if it was night or day, I was constantly looking over my shoulder. Fear seized me at every opportunity. I was honestly scared for my life. My thoughts were consumed with knives, strangers, and back alley confrontations. My fear seemed almost irrational, but as I look back

> Search me, O God, and know my heart; test me and know my anxious thoughts. See if there is any offensive way in me, and lead me in the way everlasting.
>
> PSALM 139:23-24

on it now, it took me a long time to recover from being terrorized in the park.

Fear has an eerie, slithering way of wrapping its slimy tentacles around vulnerable minds. Fear doesn't care if your concerns are legitimate or not. It feeds on terror, panic, doubt, intimidation, anxiety, lies, imagination, insecurity, catastrophe, and wild, untrue scenarios. Like a cheap, opportunistic thief, fear will rob you of your peace in Christ quicker than you can scream for help. And, too, it can systematically dismantle your relationship with God by keeping your attention fixed on horror rather than on your heavenly Father.

Whatever kind of fears you may be fighting, choose your thoughts wisely. You have the capacity to win the battle of your mind. One of Satan's most effective strategies is to use fear to get your focus off God. You can control your fears by allowing the Holy Spirit to guide how you think and what you think. The Holy Spirit will separate the truth from the lies of Satan's flaming, fear-filled arrows.

Ask God to search your heart. Ask him to test your anxious thoughts. Ask him to uproot any fear that's trying to dig its way into your life. Whether you fear walking into a classroom filled with four hundred people, moving away, confronting a new roommate who's drinking too much, losing your high school friends, not having enough money for rent, or entering your house after a scary movie, ask your heavenly Father to replace your fear with courage.

Don't waste your life by filling it with fear. Choose your thoughts wisely. God promises to lead you out of the dark alleyways of your most terrifying fears. He understands your thoughts, insecurities, doubts, and craziest imaginations. Though your fears may seem irrational and crazy to you, they're not crazy to God. He wants you to rest in his arms. He will lead you in the way of everlasting life. He'll even miraculously give you his peace as you sit on a park bench during the scariest moment of your life.

The Stand

What kinds of wild thoughts tend to occupy your mind? What types of fears are you most vulnerable to? What experiences in your past have created present fears? Think about how you think and how fear is triggered in your mind. Exposing your fears by talking to someone who cares is one of the most positive ways to get rid of them. Find someone you can talk to today about your fears. Write down three specific things you'd like to think about instead of your fears. How can you choose your thoughts wisely when you're tempted to give in to your fears?

12

OVERCOMING OBSTACLES

The Scene

Mount Whitney is the highest peak in the contiguous United States. Climbing this 14,498-foot mountain rising out of Lone Pine, California, is a serious twenty-two-mile, high altitude, oxygen-depriving trek. Climbing six thousand feet on two-and-a-half hours sleep is enough to make you hurl your apples and water all over the trail at fourteen thousand feet (take it from a puking pro).

On my first attempt of Mt. Whitney last year, friends and I encountered rain and hail at fourteen thousand feet. Rather than becoming human lightning rods, three of us decided to turn back even though the peak was only a mile away. This year, I was ready to make a two-day backpack trip a one-day siege assault.

My brother Neil and I arrived at Whitney Portal eager to prepare for our one-day hike to the top of Mt. Whitney and back. After setting up camp, we started making our evening meal. Since carbohydrates are needed for long distance endurance activities, we made rotelle pasta with Ragu vegetable spaghetti sauce wrapped in whole wheat flour tortillas. I had been hiking, running, and training for Mt. Whitney for two months, so in our last blast before taking off, I wanted to make sure I had a massive carbo load.

As Neil and I enjoyed the majestic beauty of the surrounding pine trees and the sweeping, vertical rocky slopes of Whitney Portal, we gobbled down our Italian/Mexican food combo. After two big helpings, Neil proclaimed, "I'm stuffed." I was also full, but I figured three of these packed pasta powerbars could only help for tomorrow's journey. I made myself another, downed it, and topped it off with a banana for dessert (threw in a quart of water, too!).

We cleaned our dishes, slipped into our sleeping bags at eight o'clock and set our watches for 3:45 A.M. After an hour of rolling in my sleeping bag trying to get to sleep, my stomach awoke with a churning vengeance. I couldn't remember the last time I had eaten so much. For the next four-and-a-half-hours, I twisted and turned, praying for just a few minutes of sleep. Like a dozen snakes writhing in my stomach, my carbo load turned into an indigestion nightmare.

When our watch alarms went off at the preset hour, I rolled over and groaned at Neil, "Neil, I don't know if I can make the hike. My stomach's killing me. I've had less than two hours sleep." My mind debated back and forth: *Should I give up before even starting? What about all the training I've done? I didn't make it to the top last year . . . am I not going to make it again?*

I finally willed myself to get up, get dressed, and get on the trail. "I have to at least try," I coached myself. Two hours later, a beautiful pink sunrise greeted Neil and me, the rays of the early morning sun dancing off the massive, gray granite peaks above us. The hissing snakes in my stomach finally settled down and we continued our trek to the top.

The slice

Do you tend to focus on obstacles? Do you allow pesky irritations, fears, and frustrations to get in the way of your faith? What kinds of barriers block you from following Christ? After blowing it or giving in to temptation, are you the kind of person who prays for forgiveness four, five, six times? Do you let snakes keep you from hiking the trail before you?

Someone once told me that sin is like tripping over a rock on a path. Instead of praying for forgiveness and asking God to move the rock out of our way, we focus on the rock instead of Christ. We look at the obstacle we just hit instead of allowing God to kick it off the path.

"You stupid rock! Who put you there? Look at my big toe! It's bleeding. How many other people have you tripped up? I hate rocks like you." Blah, blah, blah. On and on we blather instead of accepting God's forgiveness and moving on. Excessive shame and guilt over our sin can be major obstacles to growth in Christ. Guilt can keep you from moving along the path on which God is guiding you. Guilt can keep your focus on yourself instead of Jesus; yet his blood is more than sufficient to kick rocks and guilt out of your path.

The Christian life is like a long, slow journey up Mt. Whitney. It's filled with beautiful skies, steep paths, narrow trails, peaceful lakes, dangerous weather conditions, and breathtaking views. It's exciting. Scary. Exhausting. Dangerous. Thrilling. Your journey as a Christian is not a short, flat 5k fun run. It is a journey that will last a lifetime. A journey that will require you to look at what's ahead and not at what's at your feet.

Fixing your eyes on Jesus is a critical discipline to develop when obstacles are blocking your path. The writer of Hebrews says to fix your eyes not on obstacles but on the object of your faith, Jesus Christ. He is the author of your faith. Your faith begins, continues, and finishes in him. If the cross had been the only thing Jesus was looking at when he chose to die a slow, violent death, he might have chosen a different way. Instead of looking at the cross as an obstacle, however, Jesus saw it as a sacrificial opportunity to set the world at peace with God. He looked past the cross. He didn't fix his eyes on the pain and shame of the cross; he fixed his eyes on the throne of God. He fixed his eyes on extending his love and grace to you. Fix your eyes on receiving his grace, love, and forgiveness.

The Stand

What are the "rocks" you usually trip on? Do you freely receive God's grace and forgiveness or do you start screaming at the rock? In what area of your life do you need to fix your eyes on Jesus? How can fixing your eyes on Jesus make a difference in your relationship with him? Go for a hike today and enjoy God's beauty in creation. Just watch out for snakes!

EXCUSE ME!

Will That Be Cash, Check, or Charge?

WHAT'S YOUR PRICE?

The Scene

I had twenty one-dollar bills in my pocket, a handful of change in my right hand, and a glass filled with six raw eggs in my left hand. "Who wants to make some money?" I yelled to the roomful of high school students. Eyeing the raw eggs and the sneaky look on my face, only a few enthusiastic students screamed, "I do! I do!"

Jim, a blond-headed senior sitting next to me, stood up and asked what he needed to do to make some fast bucks.

"Jim, I have six raw eggs that I want you to drink," I said, beginning my explanation. "I'll give you a nickel for drinking six raw eggs."

"No way!" Jim protested amidst cheers and sickening groans.

"Okay," I continued, "I'll give you a dime to drink six raw eggs."

"A dime? That's it?" he exclaimed.

I threw in another nickel. "Six raw eggs . . . I'll give you fifteen cents."

"Drink! Drink! Drink!" came a roaring chorus of chants from the eager crowd.

"All right, Jim, I'll give you nineteen cents," I shouted, increasing my offer.

"Okay, you've got a deal," Jim cried as he grabbed the glass of six gooey, sticky eggs and chugged them down in three big gulps.

Cheering and screaming, the crowd went wild. Some girls looked like they were going to vomit. Then I pulled the cash out of my pocket and began counting. *One . . . two . . . three . . .* finishing my count of twenty one-dollar bills, I turned to Jim and said, "Jim, here's the twenty dollars I was willing to pay you to drink six raw eggs, but you sold out too early. Here's your hard-earned nineteen cents. Thank you very much."

The slice

The devil led him up to a high place and showed him in an instant all the kingdoms of the world. And he said to him, "I will give you all their authority and splendor, for it has been given to me, and I can give it to anyone I want to. So if you worship me, it will all be yours." Jesus answered, "It is written: 'Worship the Lord your God and serve him only.'"

LUKE 4:5-8

I was prepared to pay Jim twenty dollars to drink six gross, raw eggs! He understood the consequences. He also had a crowd. He was willing to swallow six raw eggs for a measly nineteen cents. He had his price; he simply sold out much too early.

One of my strongest reasons for writing this book is that I've seen far too many students leave their faith in Jesus Christ after high school. They sell out early. They sell out for a whole lot less than nineteen cents. It's as if they leave God in their lockers after graduation.

Graduating away from God after high school is one of the costliest mistakes you could ever make. Trading a meaningful, intimate relationship with God for the temporary success of the world isn't worth six stinking raw eggs. As you've seen by Jim's example, he had his price. Everyone has a price. What's your price?

The devil asked Jesus to name his price. Showing him all the kingdoms of the world in an instant, Satan promised Jesus power, prestige, and popularity. Anything Jesus wanted . . . all he had to do was name his price. All Jesus had to do was worship Satan. All he had to do was sell out early.

One way to strengthen your relationship with God is to be aware of Satan's temptations. You have a spiritual enemy and he has a pocketful of tricks to get you to sell out early in your faith. Refuse to sell out to Satan. Don't trade the temporary pleasure paraded in front of you for pocket change. Every day, sell out to Jesus. Count the cost of following God. Jesus paid the price for your sin by his death on the cross. Jesus counted the ultimate cost for you.

The Stand

Consider the question, "What's your price?" What would tempt you the most to sell out early in your faith? What temptations does Satan use to pull you away from Jesus? Study Luke 4:1–13 and discover how Jesus fought off the temptations of Satan. Ask God to give you wisdom to resist Satan's temptations. Thank Jesus for paying the ultimate price for your sin.

14

YOUR THREE MOST IMPORTANT
INVESTMENTS

The Scene

Every day of your life you make investments. You make investments with your time, your talents, and your money. Though you may not be sinking every paycheck into stocks, certificates of deposit, or mutual funds, everything you do is an investment. *Your life is an investment.* The important question to ask yourself is, "What am I investing in?"

This world's idea of true success is your personal net worth—that means what you're worth in dollars and cents. You flip open *Forbes* magazine and read about Bill Gates, the richest man in America who is "worth" twelve billion dollars. Next on the list is Warren Buffet, coming in a close second at a net worth of nine billion dollars. Pick up a copy of the *Wall Street Journal* and you'll find thousands of investment opportunities, all to help you increase your bottom line, your personal net worth.

Money, it seems, is the measuring stick by which your worth as an individual is determined.

For the next fifty or sixty years of your adult life, you will be challenged to define how important your net worth is to you. You'll have to consider what you choose to invest in. You'll need to think about what ultimately matters to you. Will you spend the majority of your life investing in money—or people? What will your bottom line be? Eternal matters of God or temporary, high-risk investments? Remember, your life is an investment. What are you investing in? That's worth thinking about.

The Slice

God has given you three important resources for you to make eternal investments with your life. In fact, every person in this world has been given the same three resources to make a difference for the kingdom of God. What are they?

Time: 365 days a year, 12 months, 168 hours in a week, 24 hours in a day, 60 minutes of every hour, 60 seconds of every minute. Everyone has been given the same amount of time. As you think about making eternal investments with your life, ask yourself, "What do I do with my time?"

"Then the righteous will answer him, 'Lord, when did we see you hungry and feed you, or thirsty and give you something to drink? When did we see you a stranger and invite you in, or needing clothes and clothe you? When did we see you sick or in prison and go to visit you?' The King will reply, 'I tell you the truth, whatever you did for one of the least of these brothers of mine, you did for me.'"

MATTHEW
25:37-40

Talent: In varying degrees, everyone has talents, abilities, and special gifts. Using your talents to serve God is the best investment you could ever make with your life. Serving others with your talents reaps wonderful returns in others' lives—and your own.

Money: Again, in varying degrees, everyone has money. How much money you have isn't as important as what you do with it. Understanding that the Lord is the giver and source of all your hard-earned cash will help keep you from holding on to it too tightly.

The story of the sheep and the goats in Matthew 25 is a story about investments. It's a challenge to invest in the lives of others.

> *When the Son of Man comes in his glory, and all the angels with him, he will sit on his throne in heavenly glory. All the nations will be gathered before him, and he will separate the people one from another as a shepherd separates the sheep from the goats. He will put the sheep on his right and the goats on his left.*
>
> *Then the King will say to those on his right, "Come, you who are blessed by my Father; take your inheritance, the kingdom prepared for you since the creation of the world. For I was hungry and you gave me something to eat, I was thirsty and you gave me something to drink, I was a stranger and you invited me in, I needed clothes and you clothed me, I was sick and you looked after me, I was in prison and you came to visit me."*
>
> —MATTHEW 25:31-36

It's a startling reminder that opportunities are all around you to make an eternal difference in the lives of your friends, your family, and even the lives of strangers.

When you stand before Jesus someday, it really won't be an issue of how much time, talent, or money you had on earth. Jesus will ask you, "What kind of investments did you make with your life? How did you invest what I gave you?" You don't have to be Warren Buffet or Bill Gates to make major investments in the lives of the people around you. Anything you do in the name of Jesus with your time, talent, and money will be an eternal investment worth making. Don't forget: *Your life is an investment . . . what are you investing in?*

The Stand

Your time, talent, and money are the three most important investments you can make with your life. Taking the giant step of living for God begins with investing in eternal matters. In the space below, write down three eternal investments you want to make this week:

I will invest my time in eternal matters by . . .

I will invest my talents in eternal matters by . . .

I will invest my money in eternal matters by . . .

15

CREDIT CARD CHAOS

The Scene

As you stand in the long line at the bookstore in your first semester of college, beware of free sipper bottles, spongy koosh balls, knife sets, or long distance phone minutes piled high on long folding tables. All you have to do to receive your "free gift" is fill out a little form to receive your very own Visa, Mastercard, American Express, or Discover credit cards. These free gifts are anything but free. They're silly come-ons to get your name punched on a little piece of plastic which acts as invisible money you probably don't have.

Two months later, no koosh ball is going to help you pay off the five-thousand-dollar debt you racked up. At a twenty-one-percent interest rate and minimum-wage-paying job, you've just created a fiscal nightmare the size of the national deficit. Let's see what kind of payment plan your credit card company has worked out for you.

So far, your koosh ball and credit card has bought you:

Mountain bike *(how else are you going to get to class?)*	$720.00
Macintosh computer (with printer and software)	3,500.00
Two 100 percent cotton university sweatshirts	80.00
Coffeemaker	50.00
Toaster oven with built-in cappuccino maker	50.00
Assorted posters and plants (which will quickly die)	200.00
Ugly used sofa, chairs, and "must have" lava lamp	200.00
School books *(sold back to bookstore at ridiculous rates)*	150.00
3.5 pizza dinners *(the other half is molding in the fridge)*	50.00
Total:	**$5,000.00**

Five thousand dollars at 21 percent equals $1,008.33 in interest debt. That's a total debt of $6,008.33. If you decide to pay the credit card company's minimum payment of sixteen or so dollars a month, then you'll only be attacking the interest portion of your debt. At that rate, you'll never get to the principal of your debt. As I'm sure you can see, paying only the minimum interest payment is financial slavery, but let's assume you want to take a bigger stab at paying this debt off: If you only have a hundred dollars every month to contribute to lowering your credit card debt, it will take monthly payments of $100.83 every month for the NEXT FIVE YEARS to pay off your $6,000.83 debt. Why not just go out and buy a koosh ball for two bucks? You'll save a lot of money.

The slice

"Pay back what you owe me!"

MATTHEW 18:28

Getting into credit card debt is pure chaos. Almost any company in the world will let you buy things on credit or lay-away because it's a great way to make money. Turning eighteen provides you with all kinds of new freedoms, but debt means you're not free. You're owned by a company. You've sold yourself to them for a product you purchased. Until you pay the company back, you're not free.

My sister had a roommate in college who charged over ten thousand dollars worth of stuff on credit cards. Surrounded by lots of other young students with lots of nice things, she felt pressured to keep up with them. It probably took her years to pay off the debt she had accumulated. Nothing she bought could help her dig her way out of debt. What starts with a simple free sipper bottle can turn into a serious, compulsive spending problem.

Credit card companies are students of human nature. They know that the majority of consumers buy things on whims and impulses. The principle of immediate gratification, the inability to say "no" to something you desperately want, produces a billion-dollar industry. In the 1994 Christmas season, U.S. consumers put six billion dollars on credit cards. Six billion dollars! And that doesn't include the additional billions of dollars these companies will generate from the interest!

If you want at least a million dollars worth of free financial consulting, check out God's Word. The Bible contains more verses about money than it does about love, salvation, or forgiveness. Credit card chaos can hurt your relationship with Jesus because of all the problems it creates. Instead of prayers of praise, credit card chaos will lead you to prayers of desperation, "Lord, if you just get me out of this one, I promise . . ."

Using credit cards irresponsibly can clog your relationship with God by having stuff in the center of your life instead of Jesus. Credit card companies only give you a fifteen-day grace period, but God offers you his grace for your entire lifetime. It's easier to receive forgiveness for your sins (which isn't to be taken lightly) from God than to be freed from paying a debt you can't repay. Credit card companies aren't very forgiving. They'll never die for you. In fact, if you have a bill outstanding when you do die, they'll go after your family or your estate. All that for a little koosh ball.

The Stand

If you want complete financial freedom after high school, don't underestimate the dangers of credit card debt. Refuse to slap down the plastic and buy things on impulse that you really can't afford. Before you go for the free sipper bottle or the twenty-minutes of long distance service to call your out-of-state sweetheart, read the fine print. Talk to your mom or dad about how to use credit cards responsibly. Don't enter the chaos of credit card debt. It's a trap you'd best avoid.

16

STRANGLED BY STUFF

The Scene

Cartier. The Gap. The North Face. Ralph Lauren. Nord-strom. The Sesame Street Store. Store after store tantalized my wandering eyes as I strolled through the South Coast Plaza, one of the largest, most exclusive and expensive shopping malls in the world. "This place is amazing," I said to myself as I passed beautiful window displays, exquisite jewelry, gushing waterfalls, high fashion, pencil-neck mannequins, and carefully positioned "After Christmas SALE" signs. Everything I saw inside this monstrous material-madness-filled mall was waiting for me and my dollars. Scratch that—not me, just my dollars.

Every store, every THING I passed screamed for my attention. "See me! Touch me! Feel me! You really need me . . . BUY ME! Take me home!" *Everything appealed to my physical senses.* I first tried on clothes that were comfortable and made me look good (I thought). Then I spent fifteen minutes sitting in the Panasonic Shiatsu Chair. *Aaahh!* The Shiatsu Massage Chair is a horizontal Jacuzzi-feeling, body-kneading, spine-thumping, neck-cracking, feet-tickling chair that beats you up for only $3,495 (I'll stick to my daughter's knee drops to my chest).

After getting kneaded like the Pillsbury doughboy, the intoxicating smell of fresh roasted coffee floated into my nostrils from a nearby espresso bar. Next to the espresso bar, another weakness of mine: hot, sweet-n-sticky cinnamon rolls. If I couldn't afford a chair to pummel me like dough, a steaming hot, sticky, sugar-coated cinnamon roll was the kind of dough I could afford.

The slice

Though scrumptious sweet-n-sticky cinnamon rolls taste delightfully sinful, you'll probably never hear a minister preach about the evils of pastry dough. Neither will you ever hear about an outright ban on Shiatsu massagers or glittering shopping malls. When it comes to loving the "things of this world," God's Word is clear on one thing: Stuff is not the problem; we are the problem. As human beings, we tend to have a love affair with stuff. We are strangled by stuff. A lot of times, we love things more than God. Things we can touch and feel. Things that entertain us. Things that bring us satisfaction. Things to provide us with an invisible sort of warm comfort. Kind of like a security blanket, but different. In the Old Testament,

> Do not love the world or anything in the world. If anyone loves the world, the love of the Father is not in him. For everything in the world — the cravings of sinful man, the lust of his eyes and the boasting of what he has and does — comes not from the Father but from the world.
>
> 1 JOHN 2:15-16

God told his people not to worship idols. Stuff like golden calves and carved images of tiki gods. The only difference with our idol worship today is that the golden calf now has an engine in it. A gold Lexus? Some things never change.

John, one of Jesus' original twelve disciples, dealt with the problem of Christians getting strangled by stuff by saying, "Listen, you've got to choose whom you're going to love." It's interesting what he says next. John doesn't go on a righteous rampage preaching against the dark, sinister forces of cinnamon rolls or first-century back massagers. John knows that stuff is not the problem. Stuff is not sinful. What does he say gets us in trouble?

1. The cravings of sinful man. What pulls us away from God but our cravings for something else? Our cravings are our hungers and thirsts that we try to satisfy by anything other than a fulfilling, meaningful relationship with God. Our cravings can convince us that our soul can't be satisfied with God and God alone.

2. The lust of his eyes. Walking through South Coast Plaza, my eyes were captivated by almost everything they zeroed in on. Lust is wanting to possess something in the wrong way. Lust is not just an unrestrained sexual thought about hopping in bed with a gorgeous girl or guy. It has to do with an excessive desire to own and possess anything that is not rightfully ours. When lust begins to motivate our thoughts and decisions, a dark shadow quickly cloaks our view of God. It's like putting sunglasses on our soul.

3. The boasting of what he has and does. It's not uncommon to hear words like these from new graduates: "Look at this new credit card my folks gave me for school ... it's got a five thousand dollar limit!" "Check out the new car I got for graduation." And on and on. In one way or another, we've all boasted about some new toy we have or a recent accomplishment we've succeeded in. Instead of boasting in God, we boast in ourselves (see 1 Corinthians 1:31).

So what is John asking you and me to do? It's really very simple: Love God with all our heart, soul, mind, and strength. Material things will never fulfill the deepest desires or cravings in your heart. That's a place only God can fill. Loving God brings true, lasting satisfaction. Loving God will bring you far more than material success. Loving God will keep you from being strangled by stuff.

The Stand

Do you tend to love things more than God? What is at the root of possessing things rather than developing a deeper love for Jesus Christ? Take some time to read the story of the sower and the seed in Mark 4:2–20. Write down three ways material things can choke your relationship with God. Next, write down three things you can begin to do to cultivate a richer relationship with God. Ask God for the strength to love him more than stuff.

EXCUSE ME!'

But I Wouldn't Trade Jesus for the World!

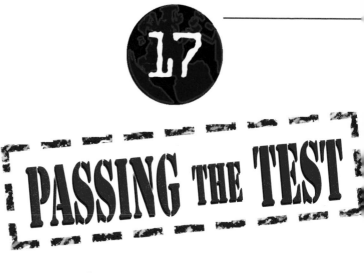

The Scene

John and Steve were two of the most active seniors in our high school youth ministry. Both of them were friendly, good-looking, popular, and admired by everyone else in the group as solid, stable, growing Christians. John had been a Christian throughout junior high and high school. Steve was previously known on campus as a heavy partier who got loaded all the time. Before Steve became a Christian, I spoke with him a number of times about how I gave up drugs and drinking to follow Christ. Steve, always with a wide-cracking grin on his face, would reply, "That's OK for you, but this Christianity stuff ain't for me. Nothing can compare with smoking a big, fat joint." When the smoke cleared, however, Steve finally realized his need for Jesus Christ.

As a young entrepreneur during high school, John had developed a small, successful floral business. After John and Steve graduated from high school, John's company quickly expanded as he acquired major accounts with local supermarkets. Needing more help with his business, John asked Steve to be his business partner. Within a short period of time, their floral business didn't just blossom . . . it exploded. As more and more money came in, John and Steve soon moved out of state to expand their business. With a flourishing flower business, their priorities about what mattered most suddenly changed. Their relationships with God soon began to wilt. Eventually, John and Steve quit doing business with God. Occasionally, somebody would ask, "Hey, how are John and Steve doing in their business?"

"They just bought a new Porsche," came the telling reply.

"Oh. Sounds like they're doing OK."

In the world's eyes, John and Steve were doing great. Making over a hundred thousand dollars a year isn't exactly tip money from waiting tables. At nineteen and twenty years old, John and Steve were making more money than most adults twice their age. However, their financial success came at the costly price of cutting off their relationship with Jesus Christ. Instead of continuing in a vibrant, growing friendship with God, John and Steve chose a temporary form of material success that appeared fruitful on the outside, but at the roots was dead and lifeless.

The slice

The Bible offers specific principles for eternal success. These principles for success begin with having God at the center of your life. Not yourself. Not money. Not Porsches. Not flowers. In God's eyes, successful living begins and ends with pursuing an authentic, growing relationship with Jesus Christ. Jesus Christ belongs in the center of your heart, your life, your relationships, and your decisions. Not out of state. Not in an ATM machine.

So what does it take to be successful in God's eyes? How can you be the person God wants you to be? Joshua was a young man chosen by God to lead the Israelites into the Promised Land. God gave Joshua specific principles for success which can make a practical and eternal difference in your life today.

> Be strong and very courageous. Be careful to obey all the law my servant Moses gave you; do not turn from it to the right or to the left, that you may be successful wherever you go. Do not let this Book of the Law depart from your mouth; meditate on it day and night, so that you may be careful to do everything written in it. Then you will be prosperous and successful.
>
> JOSHUA 1:7-8

There is nothing inherently wrong with having lots of money, nor did John and Steve walk away from God because of their financial success. John and Steve became distracted; their priorities changed, and then they abandoned their relationship with God. When you become distracted by standards of success that are different than God's, your faith is weakened. When your faith weakens, you lose the courage to keep following Christ each and every day. It takes tremendous strength and courage to keep walking with Christ after high school. Just like God said to Joshua, "I will never leave you nor forsake you" (Josh. 1:5), God promises to always be with you. He will give you the strength and courage to keep following him.

Nobody graduates from high school without passing tests. For the past twelve years, you've studied for every imaginable type of armpit-wetting test. *Knowing* what's on a test and actually *passing* the test are two different things. As a Christian, you will face tests for the rest of your life. It is possible to know the Bible without ever obeying it.

Knowing God's Word gives you the foundation you need to apply it to your life, but applying God's Word in obedience to him is something that God can't do for you. He leaves those critical decisions to you. However, he will give you the strength to make the right choices. Being a success in God's eyes is obeying and applying his Word in every situation, every day, for the rest of your life. So the real question then is . . . are you willing to keep taking tests?

The Stand

As a high school graduate, what are the greatest challenges facing you right now? (Having to sit through 683 repetitions of **DAH—DAH-DAH-DAH—DAH-DAH** does not count. Every graduate gets pummeled with Pomp and Circumstance!) How can God's power help you to be "strong and courageous" in facing these challenges? How can knowing and applying God's Word to your life assist you to successfully overcome these tests of your faith? Who can help you with these challenges? What specific step will you take this week to smack these challenges right between the eyes?

DECLARE YOURSELF

The Scene

"Tell us where the drugs are," the cop shouted at the cowering, quivering lady on the couch. "Don't be lying to us . . . you see this man right here? This man is a minister. *A preacher.* You wouldn't lie right in front of a preacher, would ya? Where're the drugs?"

The "preacher" was my friend, Chris Marshall, and the lady sitting on the couch looked thoroughly scared and confused. Should she lie or tell the truth? Was this young, blond-haired guy wearing a police chaplain's jacket really a minister? Lie to a preacher? That's like lying to God . . . what should she say?

A few weeks earlier, Chris was asked to be a police chaplain in the town where he lives on the central coast of California. Police chaplains are commonly needed during crisis situations and unique truth-telling sessions like Chris was now experiencing. Chris was what you might call "leverage."

After pulling on a bulletproof vest and brightly colored chaplain's jacket, Chris got in the front seat of the police cruiser to assist in his first drug bust. To gain entry into the suspect's house, the police officer stealthily approached the residence . . . by roaring the squad car up the lawn and onto the front porch!

The scene was pure chaos. Guns drawn. Cops running all over the place. Doors rammed down. People screaming. The only thing missing was the *Top Cops* video cameras. Chris was strategically placed to elicit the truth, the whole truth, and nothing but the truth from the suspected criminals. I don't know how Chris stood there without laughing. He is one of the most easygoing, nonaggressive people I know. Picturing him trying to keep a straight face is like trying not to laugh when your best friend accidentally burps in front of the guy she wants to date.

Since my youth, O God, you have taught me, and to this day I declare your marvelous deeds.

PSALM 71:17

The slice

Though Chris was used to get the drug suspect to declare the truth, about eight months later, Chris was faced with a serious declaration himself. After serving as a chaplain, Chris was asked to join the force. Since the police chief offered to pay for the police academy costs, Chris decided to become a police officer. While in the police academy, Chris's drill sergeant discovered that he was a former chaplain. One day when all the cadets were standing at attention, the sergeant got right into Chris's nostrils and screamed,

"Marshall!"

"*YES SIR!*" Chris screamed back.

"I heard that you were a police chaplain. Is that true?"

"YES SIR!"

"You're not one of those born-again Christians, are you, Marshall?"

"SIR! YES SIR!!"

The drill sergeant kept staring Chris down, looking for any sign of weakness, his penetrating eyes waiting for Chris to falter. What more did he have to say? Chris didn't flinch an inch. The sergeant walked away.

One of the most definitive steps to success after high school is declaring your devotion to God. Declaring your allegiance before others demonstrates a clear decision to follow Christ. When you can say to anyone unashamedly, "Yes, I am a Christian," and live in a way that validates that declaration, then you have declared yourself to God. Declaring yourself to God is a high call and high privilege worthy of your life's attention.

Instead of declaring themselves for God, some high school graduates choose to defect. Most graduates who defect from Jesus Christ don't do it for intellectual reasons. They defect from Christ for moral reasons. A commitment to Jesus Christ means absolute, total surrender to Christ. If you want to follow Jesus, remember there is always a cross. Take the cross out of Christianity and you take out Jesus. You can't have one without the other.

Instead of outright defection from God, other students simply allow their faith to deteriorate. They stop going to church. They stop reading the Bible. They stop hanging around Christian friends. Instead, they start making excuses. They neglect all things spiritual. They start becoming defensive when you ask them about their walk with God. They start living like God was never very important to them in the first place. Deterioration slowly destroys a former love and passion for God. It's a sad process of decline. What about you? Has this happened to you or your friends? Have you defected? Is your relationship with God deteriorating? Have you declared yourself for Jesus yet?

The Stand

It's never too late to declare yourself for Jesus. The farther along you are in your journey with Jesus Christ, the more exciting and dangerous your journey becomes. Without declaring yourself for Jesus, it's difficult to have a long-term vision of walking with Christ each day. Pray this prayer with me today: *Dear Jesus, today I declare myself to you. I am 100 percent completely yours. Wherever you lead me, I dedicate my life to following you. Take my life and make it what you want it to be. Guide me and protect me. Give me the wisdom and strength to walk with you each day. In Jesus' name, Amen.*

TOUGH QUESTIONS

The Scene

On July 20, 1993, Donald Wyman, a Pennsylvania strip mine bulldozer operator faced the toughest question of his life: Should I cut off my leg or not? Pinned beneath a huge oak tree, Wyman's tree-clearing project turned into a life-and-death saga when the oak tree he was sawing snapped with a ferocious kick, breaking two bones in his left leg and burying his left foot into the hard packed ground.

As an avid outdoorsman, Wyman was accustomed to adverse conditions, like sleeping in minus-fifteen-degree weather without a tent, yet none so desperate as this. After an hour or so of attempting to dig himself out, Wyman concluded that nothing was going to release his smashed foot from the unyielding pressure of the massive oak. Yelling for help proved useless; there was nobody around for miles. Could he wait a few hours or more for help to arrive? Looking at his fractured, bleeding leg, Donald Wyman contemplated the dangers of going into shock. In his own words, he concluded: *I could leave my leg here and live.*

Grabbing a dull, three-inch pocket knife, Wyman sharpened it and steeled himself for the worst agony of his life. "Finally," he said later, "I decided there was no other way to stay alive. I got myself in a determined state of mind, grabbed my leg with my left hand, resolved not to pull back, and I started cutting where the bones were already broken. It hurt terribly every time I hit a nerve or vein. My muscles jumped like frog legs in a frying pan. But I kept cutting across the top. And then I cut up from underneath until the knife came through and I could pull away."

Pretty gruesome, huh? Donald Wyman saved his life by losing his left foot. Cutting through flesh, bones, veins, and arteries, his determined will to live overshadowed the difficult, permanent consequences of life as an amputee. Donald Wyman exchanged his foot for freedom. He traded death for life. If you were in his shoes, what would you have done?

The slice

Then Jesus said to his disciples, "If anyone would come after me, he must deny himself and take up his cross and follow me. For whoever wants to save his life will lose it, but whoever loses his life for me will find it. What good will it be for a man if he gains the whole world, yet forfeits his soul? Or what can a man give in exchange for his soul?"
Matthew 16:24-26

Chances are you will never face such life-threatening or life-saving decisions as Donald Wyman, but would you do anything, absolutely anything to save your life? Me? I prefer the safer sort of questions found in the popular question and answer books. Easier, safe, humorous questions like:

➡ *Would you eat a bowl of cockroaches for ten thousand dollars?*

> ⇒ *Would you trade your grandmother for marriage to a supermodel?*
>
> ⇒ *Would you rather vomit or lose bladder control in front of strangers?*

As a high school graduate, you are going to face all sorts of tough, life-and-death questions regarding your faith. A lot of these tough questions won't be very funny. Your friends, coworkers, professors, classmates, and peers will ask where you stand on all sorts of issues—tough, thought-provoking issues like AIDS, euthanasia, hunger, world peace, education, war, the homeless, politics, gun control, abortion, philosophy, sexuality, immigration, racism, et cetera, et cetera, ad infinitum. While these questions are important and demand an intelligent response, don't allow the issues of the day to distract you from daily asking yourself the toughest, most soul searching questions of all: Are you willing to lose your life to find it in Christ Jesus? What good would it be if you gained the whole world, yet lost your soul? Will you follow Jesus Christ at any cost?

Donald Wyman fought for the survival of his life. Are you willing to do anything to fight for the survival of your faith? I don't know what your life will be like after high school, but there will be times when life crashes down on you like a massive oak tree. You'll be tempted to abandon your faith. At times, the faith that sprouted and flourished in high school may not seem to work anymore. The simple promises and answers found in Scripture won't automatically bring the relief or answers you're looking for. Other questions will capture your attention. The provocative, issue-oriented questions of our day can subtly lure you from the quiet questions of God.

These will be the hard seasons in which you make the deliberate decisions of a disciple. You probably won't lose your foot, but you'll be required to make tough decisions to tough questions like Donald Wyman. You will have to decide to act on what you know to be true and not what you feel. You will have to deny yourself. You will have to pick up your cross. You will have to resist the temporary feelings of fleeing God and instead keep on following Christ. Those are tough answers to tough questions, but those are the answers to eternal life. Nobody said following Jesus Christ would be easy, but then again, nobody told Donald Wyman he'd have to choose between his leg or life.

The Stand

What kinds of tough questions are you facing that tempt you to flee rather than follow Jesus? What causes you to want to abandon God? If you're struggling with tough questions, the best thing you can do is to talk with someone who understands you and who can give you wise, godly counsel. Working through your questions can help you follow closer to Christ.

20

PIECE BY PIECE

The Scene

One day while I was walking in the Bolivian jungle of the southern Amazon basin, a twisting, scurrying line of floating leaves on the ground caught my eye. Stepping a bit closer, I discovered a long stream of ants heading back and forth holding large pieces of shredded leaves.

"Hey, Becky, check this out," I said to my missionary friend. "Look at how big these suckers are!"

Just like one of those old Humphrey Bogart jungle-type movies, where the natives tie some poor slob to a giant anthill, these South American veggi-chomping ants were over an inch long. Not the kind of ant you'd want to meet in a dark alley. I knelt down to take a closer look.

"Those ants don't mess around," Becky said. "I've seen them strip all the leaves off a huge tree overnight."

"No way!" I exclaimed. "A whole tree in one night?"

"Look at how many there are," Becky protested. "There are thousands!"

Grasping a leaf three to four times its size, each ant powered its way through the oncoming stream of ants returning for more. For minutes, Becky and I followed the stream of green as it snaked its way over and through low-lying plants, shrubs, and bushes. Creeping, crawling, huge ants. Ants all over the place. There must have been millions. The ants were slowly, systematically destroying some tree somewhere. We kept following the curving, undulating line of ants. We didn't even know where the tree was, but the ants did. They were on a mission to consume every single part of it. One leaf at a time. One bite at a time.

> So then, just as you received Christ Jesus as Lord, continue to live in him, rooted and built up in him, strengthened in the faith as you were taught, and overflowing with thankfulness. See to it that no one takes you captive through hollow and deceptive philosophy, which depends on human tradition and the basic principles of this world rather than on Christ.
>
> COLOSSIANS 2:6-8

The slice

Piece by Piece. Nibbling. Compromising. Backsliding. Wandering. Deteriorating. Straying. Disintegrating. Eating away. Whatever you call it, allowing your relationship with God to be nibbled away is the spiritual erosion you want to avoid after high school. No student I've known has ever suddenly said, "I'm not going to be a Christian anymore." That's not how most people think, and that's not how Satan works.

As Christians, there are times when we probably don't pay enough attention to Satan's deceptive spiritual war games. The Bible warns us to guard ourselves from hollow and deceptive philosophies based on the basic principles of this world. Paul's warning is clear: don't trade Jesus for the world. Watch out for the spiritual forces that threaten to destroy your relationship with God. Just like a steady stream of South American ants, Satan uses thousands of ways to nibble away your relationship with God.

If you have a true and honest desire to grow in your friendship with God after high school, you can be sure of this: Satan has a strategy and a scheme just for you. So be wise . . . watch your walk with God. First John 4:4 promises that Christ in you is greater than Satan who's trying to get at you. You don't have to live in fear of your spiritual enemy, but you do need to make sure you're not taken captive and tied to an anthill.

A good friend once asked me, "If Satan were to trip you up in any area of your life, what would it be?" That's a good, soul-searching question. It causes me to ask myself "Am I trading Jesus for the world?" It has helped me to hand over areas of temptation and weakness to the Lordship of Christ. That's a question worth asking yourself.

Trading Jesus for all the alluring, captivating things of this world doesn't happen quickly. It's a slow, deliberate, steady process of spiritual decline. A nibble here, a nibble there. Bit by bit. That's why Paul tells his friends, "Since you accepted Jesus as Lord, continue to live in him." Paul was wise to Satan's wily ways. He knew how the creepy, crawly process of compromise worked. Continuing to live and walk in Christ prevents spiritual defoliation. If you're in Christ, it's hard for Satan to get a nibble.

So how are your roots? Are they growing deeper in the soil of God's jungle? Do you have a building, growing relationship with God or is it being eaten away by the negative influence of other people? How are you growing stronger in your faith? Does thankfulness overflow from your heart by what you see God doing in your life? Or has something or someone taken you captive? Are you more captivated by Christ or the world? If ants are crawling all over your relationship with God, ask him to get the bug juice and zap those suckers away. Is there really anything better than living in Christ?

The Stand

You don't want to get tripped up after high school by trading Jesus for the world. Trade baseball cards. Trade Barbie dolls. Join a numismatic club, but don't trade Jesus for the world. Ask yourself today, "If Satan were to trip you up in any area of your life, what would it be?" What is a specific way to grow your roots deeper in Christ today?

JOEY O'CONNOR

draws his insights
from his experiences
as one of seven
rambunctious siblings
and as a church youth
director for ten years
in Laguna Niguel,
California. He is the
author of several books:

*Breaking Your Comfort Zones
and 49 Other Extremely Radical
Ways to Live for God*

*Whadd'ya Gonna Do?
25 Secrets for Getting a Life*

*Where Is God When . . .
1001 Answers to Questions Students
Are Asking*

*You're Grounded for Life!
and 49 Other Crazy
Things Parents Say*